Hurt & Healing

Another Tale of Beauty from Ashes

Jayanna Abolmoloki

BookLeaf Publishing
India | USA | UK

Made with ❤ on the BookLeaf Publishing Platform
www.bookleafpub.in
www.bookleafpub.com

Dedication

For the young and hurting;

Life will go on, and it will be *so sweet*.

Acknowledgments

I am deeply grateful to everyone who has been part of my journey from hurting to healing. I've found love and support in the most wonderful people.

A special thank you to my Husband, Erik, for loving me through the worst and the best of times. You've brightened my world by a billion lumens.

And to the readers—if you find a bit of yourselves in any of these words, please know and remember that you are loved, too.

Preface

In 2015, at only seventeen years old, I faced a devastating heartbreak that would result in me becoming a single mother. The only outlet for my pain and loneliness was writing it out, so I did. I wrote 28 pieces from my brokenness at that time. Included in this collection are only nine of those pieces. I look back at that time in my life, and different feelings rise to the surface. Although I don't identify with that pain anymore, I still want to acknowledge that it once existed and consumed me. I have to remember the dark place I clawed my way out of and the struggles I overcame. I also want to protect my past self. She was young, vulnerable, lonely, and so very lost.

Today, as I sit here and write this preface, I am whole. Ten years later, my life is abundantly blessed by the grace of God alone. I am happily married to the man of my dreams. He guards my heart, encourages my healing, and cares for my soul. My sweet daughter, the one who made me a mother, is almost nine years old. She is truly a wonderful human being. I also have a son now, who is almost six months old.

The catalyst for my transition from hurt to healing was Jesus. I was pregnant, heartbroken, and working at Dunkin' Donuts when a coworker invited me to an event hosted by North Orange County YoungLives. She said there would be free food, and that's all she needed to say. The mentors I met there changed my life forever by displaying the love of God and pouring into me. I am forever grateful to Myrna Bittar and the ministry of volunteers she leads to serve teen parents in Orange County, CA.

Hurt

A Full-Sized Bed

I bought the cups your mother had,
To make you feel at home.

You said you'd changed your mind,
And now I'm all alone.

This bed I bought is far too big,
And longs for your touch.

I'm hoping you'll come back to me,
With all that love and such.

Discarded

I was a ripe peach,
And you swallowed me whole,
With no consideration for the tree I grew from.

You showed me no love,
As you devoured my soul.

I gave and gave,
And you gladly took,
Until you hit my pit.

Then you threw me to the floor,
And continued on your way—
Never thinking of that peach again.

A Broken Vase

You approach me like I'm a broken vase,
With a cautious, gentle look on your face.
But once you bend down to examine the cracks,
The damage you caused—you take a step back.

You decide the pieces are too sharp to touch,
Too jagged, too messy, and just too much.

Will I remain shattered, a relic of your past,
Or find strength in the fractures and hold my
own glass?

Chamomile Tea

I'm drinking chamomile tea,
And it burns the tip of my tongue,
Every time I take a sip.

The pain distracts me from you, from us,
From the thought of our child on the way.

So I keep drinking, and I let it burn.

Maybe I should be like this tea—
Scalding you every time you get too close,
Every time you offer more false hope.

Every sip is a way to feel the sting of longing.
I miss the days when you were calling,
When laughter tangled with the steam.

Now it's silence that fills the space.
A low hum of memories echoing in my head,
As I sip through my solitude,
Hoping for a warmth that's long since dead.

This Ship Has Sailed

I'm a wrecked ship, but at least I've sailed.
It would take a lot of force for the waters
To turn me around.

Yet the stars whisper secrets of the shore,
Drawing me back with their gentle allure.

The salt in my wounds still stings like before,
But your beacon of light cuts through the storm.
I yearn for the calm, yet dread the embrace.

Each wave that crashes holds echoes of pain,
But beneath the chaos, new hope can remain.

So I balance my fear on the tightrope of fate,
As I ponder the risk and the love that awaits.

My Girl In Utero

She has your smile,
And she has your eyes,
And she won't have to put up
with all of your lies.

She got the best of you,
And the rest of you... is yours to keep.

She is love,
Sent from above.
She will be happy,
She'll be carefree,
She also won't have to deal with a deadbeat.

We'll dance through the days,
With laughter so sweet,
Building a life that is truly complete.

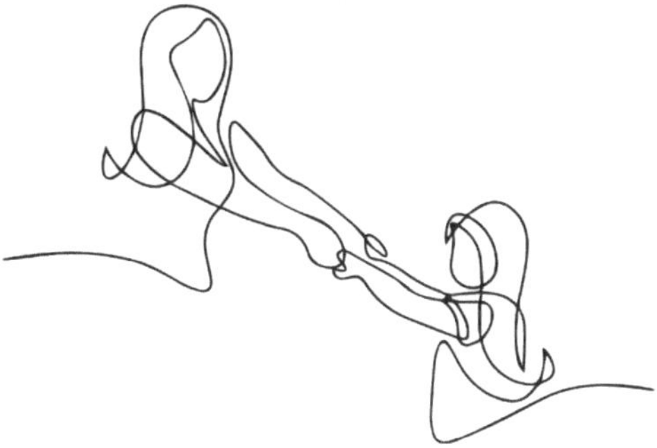

The Pursuit of Unhappiness

I was warned,
But I was dumb,
So I continued to pursue you.

I should have left you the very first time,
you hurt me like this,
But I stayed,
And I became addicted.

Because every makeup was so sweet,
It made me forget that feeling of defeat.

Mother

Hurting people hurt people—
Or that's what they say.
But to hurt your own child?
Day after day?

Holding this little love,
Staring into her eyes,
All I seem to do
Is wonder—why?

Why didn't my mother
Feel the same way?
When she held me
In her arms that day.

Couldn't she vow
To just do her best?
After holding me close,
Chest to chest.

Chains

Another bottle,
Another day.

Priorities?

Skewed, astray.

She'll drink it all down just to avoid the pain,
But does she know that she's causing the same
in the hearts of her loved ones, the ones who
remain?

Love as an action is lost on her mind,
It involves hard work—breaking chains that
bind.

But she drowned her endurance, the easier way.

And because of that choice,
stuck she will stay—

A prisoner of moments, entangled in chains.

Healing

Why?

Why would I want to be with you,
When you always cared less?

Maybe I miss myself,
Maybe I just miss our mess.

I made excuses,
To justify the let-downs.

So why,
Am I trying to get you back now?

Why would I want to be with you,
When you left me so easily?

I never would have left you,
No matter how hard staying was.

Maybe you were the weak link,
Maybe I need something stronger.

Live and be Free

What's right for me,
Isn't right for you.

It took me some time,
But I finally grew.

I see now, maybe,
What you need,
Is space to live,
And time to be free.

She and I will be fine,
With or without you.

And I want you to be happy too.

I'm forgiving,
I'm letting go,
And I hope that you'll follow
That little voice from your soul.

Forgiveness

Forgiveness is a great gift,
That was given to me.

I will slice it up,
And re-gift it to you.

And you,
And you,
And you.

Over,
And over,
And over,
Again.

Ephesians 4:31-32

Included

My God,

How incredible that You,
Included me in Your beautiful creation.

The sunshine, the soft breeze,
The flowers, the trees.

Yet You still wanted me.

How amazing,
And purely true,
The fact that,
You love me, too.

Covered in sin,
Cleansed by grace,
And saved by Your Son.

Lord, I am not worthy,
Yet You call me Your daughter,
And You treat me as if I am…

Sweet Spot

This is the sweet spot
Of life, and of love.

Resting close to You,
Basking in light from above.

Promises kept,
Of hope and a future.

Raising my children,
And loving their Father.

Redemption is sweet,
A feeling so full.

Grateful for grace,
And Your love—so whole.

My Mentor

I sat on the beach with a friend today.
I looked at her eyes as she smiled at the waves.

I noticed the way her skin tightly folded
In small little billows
At the corners of her eyes.

Her skin glistened bronze,
Like she'd been kissed by the Son.

I listened as she told me stories of her love,
Her life, her mission,
her strength, and her hugs.

My heart urged to say "Mom,"
But I held myself calm.

I looked at the waves
As they swayed and swayed,
And reminded my heart,
"It's not Mom here today."

It's a friend that I've found,
With wisdom abound,
Who shares with me willingly
As I learn to stand from the ground.

Details

Lord,

Not one of my worries
Can become a dulling overcast
that covers Your plans for me.

Thank you,

For being so concerned
With every little detail
Of my life.

. | - / *.. \\ - .

Husband

So many words
To describe his character—
So many nice things to say.

I try to write it out in a way,
Hoping that I can just maybe convey
The way real, true love feels,
The safety and security he provides.

The way that he has helped me heal,
The feeling I get when I look in his eyes.

The softness and gentleness of his touch,
Something I hadn't experienced much.

He's the only person who really knows me.
So much so, he knows when I'm hungry.

He glances over at me with love in his smile,
And asks if I haven't eaten in a while.

Children

Dishes and laundry,
Wiping and cleaning.

Diapers and shopping,
Bottles and weaning.

Doctors and Dentists,
Teachers and Speech Therapists.

Sports and art classes,
Car washes and more messes.

Children will take every moment of your life.
Every last bite, and your sleep at night.

They will crack your heart open—
But in the best way.

You'll help them grow as you watch them play,
Through laughter and chaos, their joy fills your days.

Tiny hands reaching for stars in the night,
Through whispers and cuddles, you'll cure their fright.

Toy cars and storybooks scattered around,
This is where the magic is found.

With every scraped knee, a lesson is learned.
Through Band-Aids and kisses, your own heart
is turned.

Through spills and through splashes,
Through ups and through downs,
Your family's foundation lays on solid ground.

So cherish each moment,
through the hustle and strife,
For in this sweet chaos lies the heartbeat of life.

Affirmations

I do not have to be
Anything for anyone but me.

I do not have to work so hard to please;
The audience doesn't even really like me.

I'm the best mom in the world
Because I want to be.

I'm the most loyal and loving wife
Because I want to be.

My capacity does not have to fit everyone in;
I do not have to spread myself so damn thin.

The love that I have was already earned,
And I'll nurture it well in return.

Mirror Mirror

I take a moment to look in the mirror—
A place where my bones used to shudder.

I glance at myself, my eyes, and my skin
and I say, "that's somebody's Mother."

She stares back at me with a gentle gaze
and she says, "my dear girl, look how you've
changed."

She reaches out to me and touches my face.
"You've been hard on yourself;
you deserve some grace."

I stare back at her, eyes beginning to crease
I realize it's just me—finally at peace.

Compass

You can have it all, God.

You created me,
You have guided me,
And nurtured me even when I wasn't aware of it.

So why should there be anything I covet?

I want others to take a peek at my life
And see that it points to you, Lord.

At times, life gets tough,
And I feel like I am not enough.

But You, God, redeem me
When I cannot redeem myself.

Thank you.